IMAGES OF ENGLAND

MARLBOROUGH
REVISITED

IMAGES OF ENGLAND

MARLBOROUGH
REVISITED

MICHAEL GRAY

TEMPUS

First published 2007

Tempus Publishing Limited
The Mill, Brimscombe Port,
Stroud, Gloucestershire, GL5 2QG
www.tempus-publishing.com

British Library Cataloguing in Publication Data.
A catalogue record for this book is available from the British Library.

ISBN 0 7524 3986 3

Typesetting and origination by Tempus Publishing Limited.
Printed in Great Britain.

Contents

Acknowledgments 7

Foreword 8

one The Fringes 9

two The Town 15

three The Churches 41

four Trade and Business 45

five Transport 59

six People and Events 65

seven Schools 93

eight War and Disasters 97

nine Recreation 105

ten Medicine and Law and Order 109

eleven Marlborough College 113

twelve Coronation Day 121

A Wiltshire Pig.

You may push me
You may shuv
But I'm hanged
If I'll be druv
From Marlborough.

Acknowledgments

The author would like to thank the Merchant's House (Marlborough) Trust for permission to use its photographic archive at the Merchant's House, who has been most supportive in advice and sourcing of images. Also to Harry Foster, retired librarian, for exhaustively checking and proof-reading the text.

Michael Gray
2006

Foreword

Michael Gray, the compiler of this fascinating collection of archive photographs of Marlborough, was born in the town and has lived there all his life. His passion for the traditional soul of Marlborough is evident from his sometimes trenchant captions, and he speaks with authority on the historical changes of the past 130 years. Marlborough is one of this country's favourite tourist attractions and most visitors return to explore its hidden charms time and time again. The pleasures of a window seat in the Polly Tea Rooms, a stroll along Treacle Bolly to pass under the Marlborough White Horse, or simply the charm of the numerous historic alleyways off the High Street, have been recalled and discussed by visitors from all over the world. This carefully researched selection of photographs will evoke nostalgic memories in itinerant travellers and long-term residents alike, and will remind future generations about the true nature of country town life in years long gone by.

   This is the second collection in the *Archive Photograph Series* by Michael Gray, and it contains a further 200 images of the scenes, the people and the life of the town. All the photographs come from the archives of the Merchant's House, a seventeenth-century silk merchant's house being lovingly restored to its former glory, by permission of the Merchant's House (Marlborough) Trust.

Harry Foster
2006

one

The Fringes

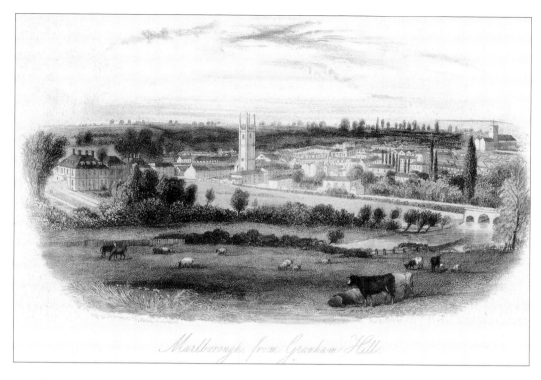

View from Granham Hill from a print, *c.* 1845. This is a fairly accurate representation showing from the left: 'C' House, Marlborough College and St Peter's church. On the right is St Mary's church with the large bulk of the Ailesbury Arms Hotel next to it.

View of the town from Postern Hill showing the unmade road to Salisbury. Beyond can be seen the railway with the station master's black-painted house prominent, *c.* 1920.

View of the town from Granham Hill.

The white horse on Granham Hill above Treacle Bolly. This was formed by the boys of Marlborough Academy in 1804. The Academy house is now the Ivy House Hotel.

A well-dressed party visiting Braydon Oak, *c.* 1910. The house, in its beautiful isolated location, is still there.

Opposite: From a postcard inscribed 'Early morning in the Savernake Forest'. Sadly, these fine beeches from the Grand Avenue had to be felled for safety reasons in the 1960s. Replacement trees were planted – close together to encourage height – and are now mature enough to require thinning.

Haymaking just outside Marlborough, *c.* 1930. (Part of Revd Harry Lane's photography collection of agricultural subjects)

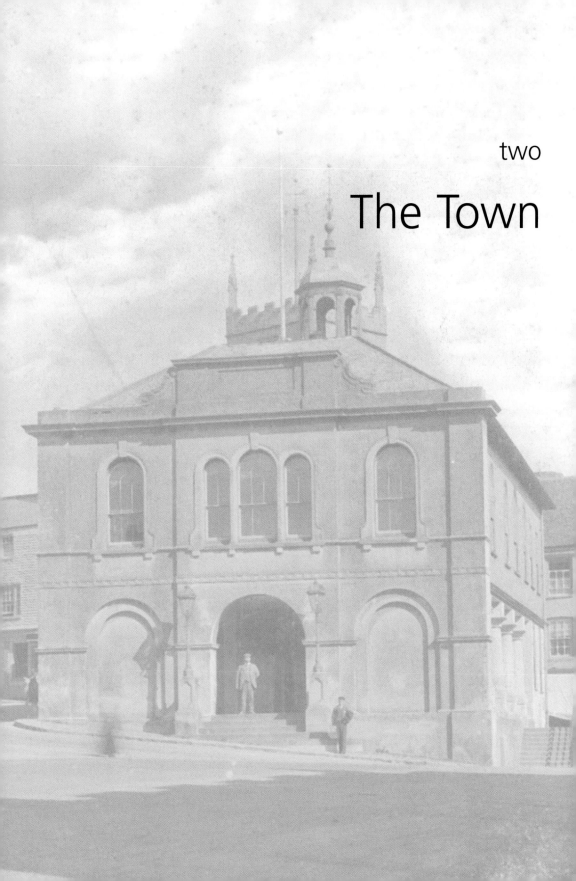

two

The Town

Marlborough from the air, *c.* 1925. To the left, the industrial buildings behind the High Street are still intact.

This view dates from around 1930. Vehicles now park in the centre of the High Street, but demand is not large. The prominent building to the left, behind the main building, is the Castle & Ball annexe, a popular venue for dances and events. This was destroyed in the 1960s to make way for a car park.

High Street from St Mary's tower, *c.* 1970. The motorway-style lamp standards have now mercifully been replaced.

A view of the corner of the High Street and Kingsbury Street showing the densely packed workshops behind the street frontages, *c.* 1970. The stone-fronted Victoria House (1840) shows an imaginative way of dealing with this narrow corner.

West end of the High Street, *c.* 1880. To the right is the Sun Inn, St Peter's boys' school and Mr W. Gale's printing office with its Georgian shop front.

WEST END OF HIGH STREET, MARLBOROUGH, SHEWING ST. PETER'S CHURCH.

High Street looking west, *c.* 1920. Mr Paice sold his bicycle business to Herbert Duck in 1926, and it has remained in the family until the present day.

High Street, *c.* 1938. In the foreground is the wicker post office handcart which was still in use in the 1950s. On the right, the brick building with stone dressings was destroyed in the 1960s. The cinema, the building to the left with arches is now a supermarket.

High Street looking to the west, *c.* 1925. The shop awnings covering the pavement are yet another feature of the town which has been lost.

Above and below: Two views of the High Street taken in May 1918. The soldier and civilian have obligingly posed for both photographs. Traffic is non-existent except for the army lorry in the view to the east.

Opposite above: View from the gates of St Peter's church looking east – before any architectural horrors had invaded the High Street – around 1930.

Opposite below: High Street to the east, *c.* 1905. This image shows the largely residential character of the St Peter's end of the street, a situation which remained unchanged until the 1950s.

The as-yet unsurfaced High Street, *c.* 1915. St Peter's school on the left has now been stripped of its attractive gates, railings and holly tree.

High Street, *c.* 1880. The buildings in the right foreground were progressively rebuilt by the Maurice family and included a residence, a surgery, flint gates leading to a stable and a coach house, with extensive gardens to the river.

High Street to the east, 1873-74. On the left is Mr Lucy's stationery shop. This photograph was taken during the brief revival of Marlborough's first newspaper – hence the signboard proclaiming 'Journal office'.

High Street, 1901-1904. The weighbridge was removed in 1925. There are hitching rails outside the Green Dragon but the drinking trough has not yet been installed.

Above: East end of the High Street and the town hall. This shows the 1867–1900 town hall frontage and the weighbridge house with the platform and lamp. Part of Free's warehouse is visible on the right.

Christopher Hughes has used one of his own pen and ink sketches in this 1921 Christmas card. Although it is 1921, Hughes is still reluctant to depict motor vehicles; almost all traffic shown here is horse-drawn.

Right: Seventeenth-century survival. Chandler's Yard (formerly Horse Passage) is now a public footpath to Back Lane, but evidence of a door at the High Street end attest to its original function as a private yard. Both sides of the passage are flanked by extensive wings built behind merchants' houses. Cavendish House, to the left, has possibly pre-fire flint courses and a surviving seventeenth-century staircase window above.

Opposite below: The 1867 town hall features in this original pen and ink drawing which dates from around 1890.

Above: The town hall in 1792. This building was demolished the following year, but the columns were re-used in both later town halls – and are still there.

Left: The re-fronted town hall of 1867. This was a stone front planted on the west façade, with the columns of the open hall behind, visible to the right. (E.H. Roberts, local photographer)

Opposite above: Town hall, south side in 1867. To the right of the building is the ground floor lock-up with staircase above.

Opposite below: The town hall under construction. Designed in 1882, building work did not begin until 1900 and was completed in 1902. Mr Hawkin's cart stands in the foreground. He was a brickmaker from Great Bedwyn. The scaffolding is lashed together with rope.

Left: The brand new town hall of 1902.

Below: The Sun Inn and St Peter's junior school, *c.* 1930.

Opposite below: To the left, the oldest secular building in town. Built around 1480, possibly as the residence for a chantry priest based in St Peter's church, it is here shown re-fronted and used as Pope's Iron Works. Next to it is a brick terrace, a re-facing of seventeenth-century properties, Nos 100-104 High Street. Only the left-hand shop now survives; the centre of the block became the new post office in 1910, the right-handed section became Boots the Chemist in the 1960s.

Above: Lucy & Co. and Bane. This fine seventeenth-century building is now open to the public as the Merchant's House. It was built for Katherine and Thomas Bayly in 1653-56. One assumes that the gathering is the workforce of Mr Lucy, or Mr Jarvis who traded under the same name until 1926.

Left: The new post office has punched a hole in the terrace shown on page 29 and is here being opened by the mayor in 1910. It is now a pizza house.

Below: The Green in the 1950s. The corner house was built by Thomas Free, and is embellished with carved woodwork by craftsmen from his furnishing business.

Opposite above: A view of the western flank of the Green and Oxford Street, *c.* 1935. The electricity sub-station is a recent addition; the planting around it is clearly new.

Opposite below: The Green, *c.* 1935. Savernake Forest has a gracious park-like appearance. The slopes are now densely covered in scrub and at their base is an incipient industrial development.

Above: A summer day on the Green in the 1920s. The Toc H symbol can be seen above the eponymous building to the right. The house next door has stone tiles on its lower roof slope – the last to be seen in the town. These were lost around 1965.

Left: Silverless Street, *c.* 1930. The trees on the right mark the position of the present car park but until comparatively recently this area was part of the Green.

Opposite below: 161 Lower Kingsbury Street; an etching by Christopher Hughes, *c.* 1930.

Above: Kingsbury Street, 1905. Little has changed since then, except fashions in children's clothes.

New Road, 1904. The road was made in 1812 to facilitate entry of stage coaches into the town. On the right is a walled garden with trees, then belonging to Wye House.

A garden at the lower end of New Road which had been utilised in the 1920s as the site for the war memorial; beyond is the parking area for Dobson's Garage which is sited across the road. Outside, the petrol pumps served directly at the roadside.

The Parade with an early parking sign on the lamp post. The gabled property on the left still bears the borough arms although the inn of that name closed in 1913. The coat of arms is still there.

The Parade in about 1930; an etching by Christopher Hughes.

Above: George Lane; Marlborough's oldest suburb. The cottages to the left centre pre-date the Great Fire of 1653, the George Inn to the right is seventeenth century. The latter was demolished in 1945 to make way for prefabs which were never built. Instead, a Nissen hut housed the Catholic church – this was replaced by a permanent building in 1959. The lane crossing the road here, from beyond the forge to the front of the George Inn, was the main entry to Marlborough from the south, crossing the river via a ford.

London Road with the Great Lamp to the left, *c.* 1920.

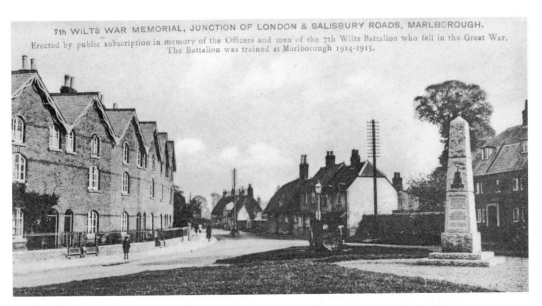

7th WILTS WAR MEMORIAL, JUNCTION OF LONDON & SALISBURY ROADS, MARLBOROUGH.
Erected by public subscription in memory of the Officers and men of the 7th Wilts Battalion who fell in the Great War.
The Battalion was trained at Marlborough 1914-1915.

Above: War Memorial to the 7th Battalion, the Wiltshire Regiment, *c.* 1920. It has since been moved to make way for the needs of the motor car.

Opposite below: George Lane looking east. The low building in the centre is a smithy. To the left is a property of random stone and flint, which is almost certainly reclaimed material from the Gilbertine Priory at St Margaret's. Its form indicates that it could have been built in the immediate post-Reformation period. The gabled and jettied structure beyond is the George Inn, which would have served drovers at this tiny settlement which was surrounded by pasture. Marlborough town started on the other side of the river Kennet.

London Road, *c.* 1910. The Five Alls public house is an Edwardian update of a mid-Georgian building.

The same view today.

The pound on the common. Animals found wandering by the herdsman would be placed here and their release cost the owners 2d for a pig and 1s for a cow, together with the cost of the animal's keep. Any beasts not claimed after four days were sold.

St Mary's Vicarage, St Martin's, built around 1840 and demolished in the 1960s to make way for the Vicarage Close development.

Seventeenth-century barn at Barton Farm, *c.* 1930. It was lost to fire
in 1976. Virtually all the rest of Marlborough's working/industrial
past has been shamefully destroyed by demolition. The police station,
the repeater station, the gas retort house, the watermill, both railway
stations, and workshops behind the High Street have all disappeared
since 1960.

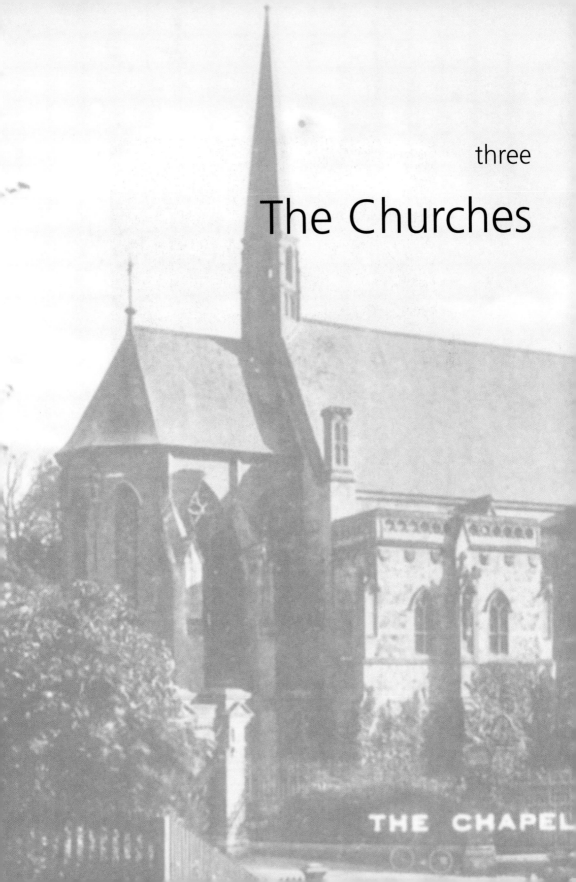

three

The Churches

THE CHAPEL

St Mary's church bells, returned after re-casting in 1922. The new steel frame is seen to right and left.

St Mary's church before the 1874 restoration, at which date a chancel was built on to the fifteenth-century nave and the oak box pews were removed. (Print by Rock & Co., London, 1861)

St Peter's church tower and the Sun Inn, the latter displaying some splendid signage, *c.* 1905. Boatered college boys are much in evidence. Notice the cobbled crossing in the unmade road.

Marlborough College chapel, built 1883–86. The architects were Bodley and Garner.

four

Trade and Business

John Duck (1842–1925). The painted sign on his workshop in Angel Yard described him as a 'Veterinary and Shoeing Smith'. This combination of skills was commonly found until well into the twentieth century.

The workforce of Howse & Milburn of No. 139 High Street, *c.* 1900. Second from left is the borough beadle.

The same view 100 years later. Changes in the beadle's antiquarian costume are noticeable. Now rendered and refenestrated, the building was a seventeenth-century merchant's two-gabled holding with panelled rooms on the first floor.

81, High Street, Marlborough, *Xmas* 190*1*
(And London Road.)

Mrs. P. Keate

Bought of A. W. BELL,
Cycle Maker, & Agent for Best Makers.

❖ REPAIRS ❖ A ❖ SPECIALITY ❖

All the Newest ACCESSORIES kept in Stock, or
promptly obtained to order.

July 5/10 Rep 2 Self Sealing Tubes	6	0
Sept 4 Set Crank & Pedal	1	0
	7	0

Paid Jan 5/02
A W Bell
With Best Thanks

Bodman's shop, *c.* 1930. Small shops were to be found in St Martin's, Silverless Street (as here), the Green and Blowhorn Street. All have now disappeared.

Opposite above: Herd & Leader and the Violet Tea Rooms, High Street, *c.* 1930. The kerbside petrol sales continued until the 1970s.

Opposite below: Billhead for A.W. Bell Cycle Agent at No. 81 High Street. Notice that he has a branch elsewhere in the town. This was quite usual until the demise of the family shop in the 1960s.

Dunford's, at No. 113 High Street, combined the retailing of boots and shoes with chocolate, just before the First World War.

JOSEPH FRANKLIN,

(LATE CHALLEN WHITE & CO).

ENGLISH & COLONIAL MEAT DEPOT.

Pork Butcher.

CELEBRATED WILTSHIRE SAUSAGES.

Corned Beef. Pickled Tongues.

MARKET PLACE, MARLBOROUGH.

Advertisement for Joseph Franklin, butcher, of No. 3 High Street, taken from *Lucy's Directory* of 1899.

Small shops proliferated until the arrival of the supermarkets in the 1960s. This is No. 77 High Street, near St Peter's church.

Three small businesses, *c.* 1955. At No. 18 is Dennis Pocock, estate agent and auctioneer; at No. 19 is D.W. Pocock, grocer, with his delivery van outside; and at No. 20 is Gantlett, the chemist (one of three in the town).

Above: No. 105 High Street, *c.* 1905. Mr Marshall's shop was later to be subsumed into the expanding Free business empire.

Opposite below: Trade card of the Angel Coffee Tavern Co. at No. 9 High Street, *c.* 1910. What a relief to know that the hotel provides lavatories.

Above: The staff of Mundy's shoe shop, 1908. This is a professional photograph taken in the yard of No. 143 High Street. Mundy's second shop was located at No. 72 High Street (north of St Peter's church), and the firm later also acquired No. 5 High Street near the Ailesbury Arms Hotel. Pictured here are, from left to right: Messrs Oslind, Shawry, Green, - ? - , Webb (seated).

The "Five Alls" Inn,
London Road,
Marlborough.

(Soldier) I fight for all.
(Priest) I pray for all.
(King) I rule all.
(Lawyer) I plead for all.
(Farmer) I pay for all.

Above: The Five Alls Inn, London Road. An Edwardian makeover of an eighteenth-century building, as shown on a postcard, *c.* 1910. The meaning of the name is explained in the top right-hand corner.

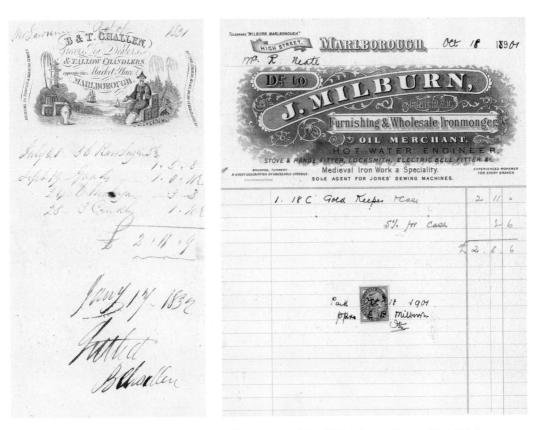

Above left: Billhead dated 1831 of Mr Challen, grocer, of No 3 High Street. Sent to Mr Elijah Lawrence, whose drapery shop was situated behind the town hall.

Above right: Billhead for J. Milburn, a highly successful ironmonger at No 139 High Street. He was one of the town's businessmen who moved out of the centre and built a grand villa on the outskirts – in this case Highfield, on the Common, now a residential home.

Opposite below: The Ailesbury Arms Hotel, complete with petrol pump and garaging, kept ahead of the motoring trend. The large first floor window to the left lit the billiards room. This image is from the auction catalogue of 1929, when the Ailesbury family sold off a large number of its properties.

These pages: Four examples from an extensive collection of photographs taken by the Revd Harry Lane in the 1930s. His studies of farm wagons are an important historical resource now that these beautiful vehicles are no more. When these pictures were taken most of the wagons were still in use.

Kennet and Avon Canal Navigation.

THIS TICKET certifies,

That *Mr Peter Green*

is a Proprietor of and is intitled to a Share in the *Kennet and Avon Canal Navigation*, made by Virtue of an Act of Parliament made and passed in the thirty-fourth Year of the Reign of his Majesty King GEORGE the Third, intitled " *An Act for making* " *a navigable Canal from the River Kennet, at or near* " *the Town of* Newbury, *in the County of Berks, to* " *the River Avon, at or near the City of* Bath ; *and* " *also certain navigable Cuts therein described,*" and of several other Acts of Parliament for completing the said Canal; and that the said Share is numbered *4239* in the Register Books of the Company of Proprietors of the said Canal Navigation.

In Testimony whereof the Common Seal of the said Company is hereunto affixed this 2d Day of *April*, in the Year of our Lord One Thousand Eight Hundred and Eight.

<small>(Harold, Printer, Marlboro'.)</small>

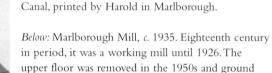

Left: A rare share certificate for the Kennet and Avon Canal, printed by Harold in Marlborough.

Below: Marlborough Mill, *c.* 1935. Eighteenth century in period, it was a working mill until 1926. The upper floor was removed in the 1950s and ground floor torn down twenty years later. The complete set of machinery was removed elsewhere. (Harry Lane – photograph from his collection of watermills in the Marlborough area)

five

Transport

Savernake Hospital and the porter's lodge. The vehicle is not an effete means of transport but a tipping dung cart, *c.* 1890.

Annual outing of Marlborough Amateur Dramatic and Operatic Society, 1928. The charabanc has pulled into the roadside somewhere between Weston-super-Mare and Cheddar Gorge for the photograph.

A view from the first floor of Mr Free's premises at Nos 104–107 High Street, *c.* 1925. The Dennis lorry is making a delivery to Ushers' (of Trowbridge) wine and spirit department. In the background the roadway is under reconstruction with the aid of a steamroller. The pretty Victorian street lamps have not yet been replaced by the hideous steel gantries of the fifties.

The 'Scout' was the only motor vehicle manufactured in Wiltshire in the early twentieth century and a great many were sold in the county. This advertising postcard of 1912 urges the recipient to '... go in for Motor Traction. We can, of course, fit any kind of body, or even supply without body.'

H. E. WALTON

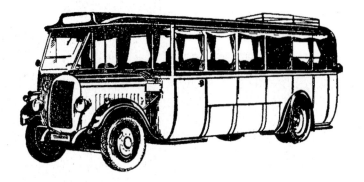

COACHES & CARS
FOR HIRE

DAIMLER CAR, 1932 Model, 16-20 h.p.
BEDFORD SUN SALOON BUS, 1933

REPAIRS

NEW ROAD GARAGE
MARLBOROUGH

PHONE 281

Advertisement for Mr Walton's hire company. His vehicles are dated to show that
he has recent models. The open charabanc shown on page 60, is of a type almost
completely replaced in the early 1930s by the enclosed type shown here, albeit with a
large sun roof.

Solid-tyred lorry belonging to Cumner's Stores, of the Parade. The main outlet for Cumner's, the principal grocery in the town, was in the High Street.

Snowed-in lorries in the High Street, winter 1962-63. These were the days when all east-west traffic passed through the town. The M4 was opened in 1971.

The reason for the reduced camber in the High Street. Several large loads (including this steel frame in around 1958) were shed on to the pavement before the levelling took place.

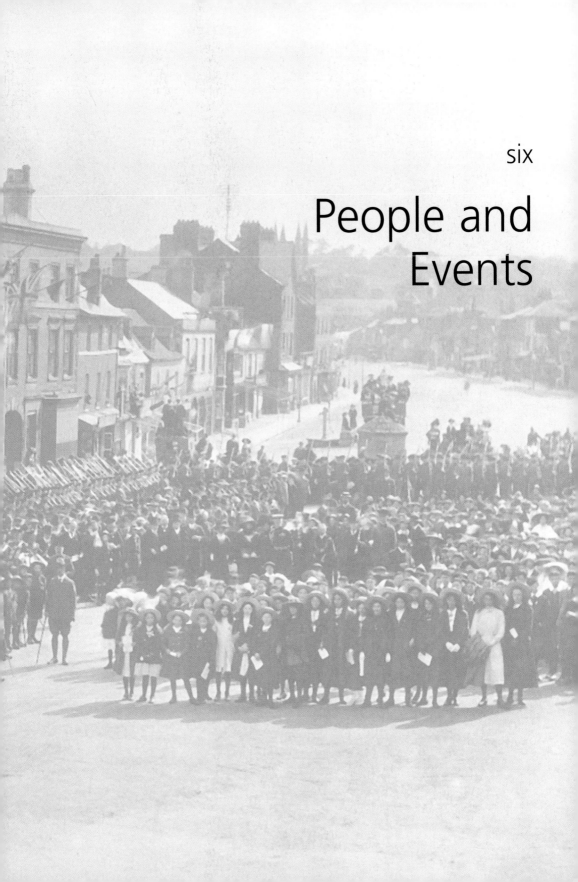

six

People and
Events

Leaves From the Maurice Family Photograph Album

The following images are leaves from the Maurice family photograph album (kindly donated to the Merchant's House archive by Mrs Ann Maurice). They date from the 1890s. The Maurice family have practised medicine in Marlborough from 1792 until the present day.

Young friends of the family. Do the rosettes and bat denote a female cricket match?

Opposite above: This image shows the Georgian Lloran House to the right with the 1880s extensions stretching to the corner of Figgins Lane. The buildings comprise an extension to Lloran House then the flint-walled entrance to the stable yard. Beyond the tree is the surgery, and lastly, the house James Maurice built for his assistant and dispenser, Dr Parr.

Opposite below: Rear view of the property. Sadly, this grandeur is now eclipsed; the greenhouse has gone and the whole lawn is covered with a clutter of ugly 1960s buildings and a car park. The Victorian oriel window survives but is difficult to see.

Pastoral idyll which is now the surgery, car parks and industrial units (and their car parks). When this photograph was taken, the Maurice land extended beyond the river Kennet to George Lane which was also undeveloped. This is looking east from the south bank.

Above left: The doctor's transport, July 1890 – a smart turn-out, seen in the stable yard. Just visible to the left is a glimpse of the north side of the High Street and Jarvis's stationery shop.

Above right: A charming and extensive view of the High Street. Beyond the weighbridge, boys have gathered around the town pump. The world is holding its breath for the arrival of motor transport.

Opposite above: The original camping holiday, 1891. Here the caravan is on the road between Marlborough and Ogbourne. The man on the right, referred to as Cox on the album's caption, was the family coach driver.

Below: Setting up camp, 1893. One assumes the attire is late-Victorian casual. Did Cox, centre, sleep in the tent?

Immaculate and elegant, these are siblings Robert, Polly and Jack Giffard from Lockeridge House. This is the occasion of the wedding of another sister, Violet, to Oliver Calley Maurice in 1901. Sadly, Violet died of TB only six years later.

Left: Oliver Calley with his bride and her brothers on their wedding day in 1901. Dr Oliver was devastated by the loss of Violet in 1906, and the whole town was shocked when he died in 1912 at the early age of forty-two.

Opposite above: Part of the Maurice family property empire, *c.* 1906. Lloran House, No. 41 High Street, is to the right. Dr James stands beside his carriage, Oliver with his children on the pavement, Thelwall in the porch. Walter is at the wheel of the motor car.

Below: Picnic at Martinsell. Sartorial standards are never relaxed, even on such an occasion as this. One suspects that there are trestle tables and family servants just out of frame.

Children's tea in the Corn Exchange, probably Coronation Day, 1911.

Opposite above: Motor car inspection in the High Street by Lord Roberts, September 1903. The military taking an interest in the latest technology.

Opposite below: Another view of Lord Roberts' inspection of motor cars, 1903. The end is in sight for horse-drawn transport such as seen here in the foreground.

MEMORANDUM,
FOR DINERS.

Each person will bring a cup, plate, knife and fork.

Dinner will be on the table punctually at one o'clock.

It is earnestly requested that diners will be careful to seat themselves at the tables for which their tickets are numbered. On account of the large number dining great confusion will be created if there is any departure from this arrangement.

After a flourish of trumpets at one o'clock, everyone will stand up while grace is sung by a choir. Another flourish of trumpets will announce the conclusion of the dinner, when grace will again be sung.

Immediately afterwards the whole company will assemble in the centre of the High-Street, and the Band will play the first half of the National Anthem. Then a short pause, after which the whole of the assembly will sing the three verses of "God Save the Queen" on a signal given by Mr. Bambridge.

PRINTED AT THE "TIMES" OFFICE, MARLBOROUGH.

Instructions for the dinner commemorating Queen Victoria's Golden Jubilee in 1887. Notice that all the verses of the national anthem are to be sung; 'frustrate their knavish tricks' is rather out of fashion today.

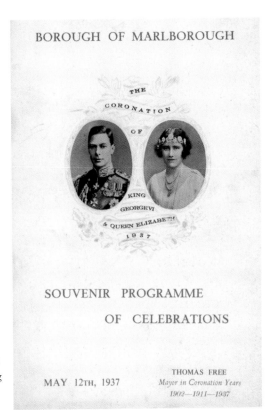

BOROUGH OF MARLBOROUGH

THE
CORONATION
OF

KING
GEORGE VI
& QUEEN ELIZABETH
1937

SOUVENIR PROGRAMME

OF CELEBRATIONS

MAY 12TH, 1937

THOMAS FREE
Mayor in Coronation Years
1902—1911—1937

Right: Cover of the Coronation programme of 1937. The day began with the firing of a gun on the common and ended with a dance in the town hall.

Below: Empire Day in the High Street, 1910 or 1911. The mayor, Thomas Free, stands behind the schoolgirls with the officers of dignity and a senior army officer. The military is arrayed along the south side of the street with Britannia on a plinth outside the Angel Temperance Hotel.

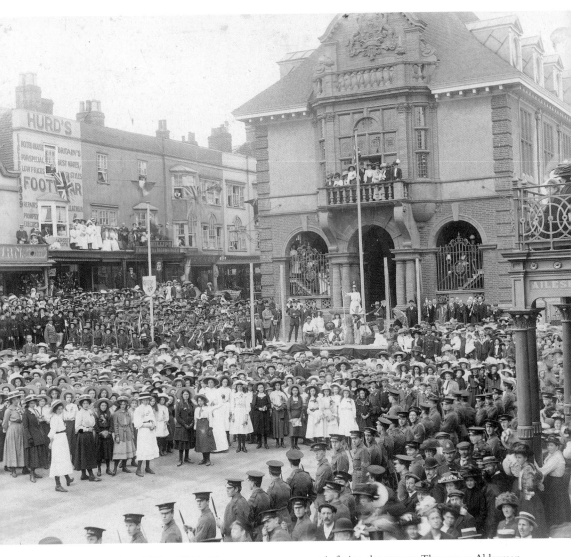

Above: Empire Day, 1910 or 1911. Almost everyone present is facing the camera. The mayor, Alderman Thomas Free, together with other municipal dignitaries, is seen to the right of the town hall portico. In the centre is a tableau representing the British Empire. Groups represented include the military, Boy Scouts and grammar school girls – the latter recognisable by the badges on their straw hats. Mr Phillips' shop was sacrificed to a new building for the Midland Bank in 1925.

Opposite above: Street party in celebration of the Coronation of King George V in 1911, outside the home of Mr W.F. Woodward, solicitor. To the left is the yard entrance to the Ailesbury Arms Hotel. This is a good documentary record of the original frontage of No. 7 High Street, which was a mid-Georgian town house. It still exists, but the entire ground floor has been altered to accommodate a modern shop front. The beautiful gas lamps were to go in 1925.

Opposite below: Coronation street party, 1911, showing the Jolly Butcher public house group, probably by the same photographer as the image above. He may have done the rounds of all the pavement groups, thus turning the day into a nice little earner.

Bonfire on the common to celebrate the Diamond Jubilee of Queen Victoria in 1897. Alderman Thomas Free is behind the perambulator.

St Martin's celebrates the end of the Second World War with a children's tea party. It is not known whether this is VE or VJ Day.

An important military visitor with the mayoral party in 1910 or 1911. As usual, Alderman Free's dog is in attendance. The interest here is that the image shows a professional photographer in action; the camera is on its tripod and the operator has his head under the black cloth.

Above left: A *carte de visite* of Elizabeth Lovell Maskelyne taken shortly before her death in 1874 at the age of thirteen. The Maskelyne family ran the printing and stationery business at No. 132 High Street from 1871-1877. Elizabeth's father wrote to his sister using the phrase 'poor Bessie is gone', suggesting that the death had come as no shock to either of them. The *carte de visite* was taken by photographer Alfred Lane of Marlborough and Pewsey.

Above right: Verso of the left image – with an advertisement for Mr Lane's business.

Left: Fred Beckingham, gamekeeper, outside his cottage in Kingsbury Terrace. His daughter Ada was born in 1901.

Below: The Wiltshire family in the garden of No. 85, London Road. This is a professional group portrait taken in September 1912, showing the well-turned-out appearance of a prosperous artisan family of the period.

Alderman Henry Cooper with Mrs Cooper and the officers of dignity. This was taken in the Council Chamber, 1933–34.

The mayoral party en route to St George's church, Preshute, 1968. In the background are the college chapel, the Memorial Hall and the pinnacles of St Peter's tower.

Above: Civic group on the town hall steps, 1952 or 1953. Alderman and Mrs Eric Free are seen with, to their right, town clerk Clifford Bell and Alderman Christopher Hughes (local topographical artist and First World War Military Cross holder) and Dr Timothy Maurice of the Marlborough medical family dynasty. Sadly, councillors no longer wear the silk hats.

Opposite below: Awaiting the arrival of the King and Queen in March 1948. The borough council and prominent citizens are assembled in the Court Room of the town hall. Behind the table are the mayor and mayoress, Alderman and Mrs James Duck. 'Jimmie', as he was known, was serving his fourth term in office. In the wig and tabs is Clifford Bell, town clerk. Standing next to the macebearer on the left is Alderman Thomas Free, now ninety-four years of age – he died the following year.

Right: His Majesty, King George VI, acknowledges the cheers of the crowd from the balcony of the town hall.

Below: The Royal Daimler (no number plate) arrives to the cheers of Miss Hutchins' cub pack.

TO THE
Worthy & Independent
ELECTORS
OF THE BOROUGH
OF
MARLBOROUGH
AND THE
PARISH OF PRESHUTE.

GENTLEMEN,

WE might expose ourselves to a charge of Ingratitude, were we not, on this the second day of our Canvass, publicly to announce to you, the high obligation we are under, for the very cordial reception and encouragement we have received at your hands.

The promises of support already tendered to us, give us, not only the highest gratification, but also the best assurance of success. Should we be returned as your Representatives, the obligation of consulting your own immediate, and local Interests, in common with the general welfare, will be more firmly fixed on our minds, by the generous confidence you have been pleased to bestow upon us, during our Canvass yesterday and to-day; and it shall be our constant endeavour to unite our best efforts to obtain for the Country in general, the great blessings of good Government, with the strictest regard to economy; and to guard over and protect, the well-being and independence of the ancient and highly-respectable Borough of Marlborough.

We remain,

GENTLEMEN,

Your much obliged and obedient Servants,

ERNEST BRUCE.
HENRY BARING.

MARLBOROUGH, 5th JULY, 1832.

EMBERLIN AND HAROLD, PRINTERS, &c., STAMP OFFICE, MARLBOROUGH.

Marlborough.

A few inquisitive friends of SIR ALEXANDER MALET, warm supporters of freedom of Election, thinking it of the first importance that men of *strict probity* and *unimpeachable character* should be alone returned to a reformed House of Commons, beg humbly to ask an early answer to the following questions.

1. Whether it can be possibly true that he went by the name, at Winchester School, of Sir Alexander Liar, Bart. ?

2. Whether he was not *expelled* from the said school. ?

3. Whether he did not *retire* from College at Oxford to save *expulsion ?*

4. Whether he did not seek employment, as a Tory, under a Tory government ? and whether such employment did not *cease* in consequence of his having been concerned in SMUGGLING, i. e. availing himself of his situation in the Foreign Office to send contraband goods to this country from Paris ?
Great anxiety is manifested for an explicit answer to this question, as, tho' hard to believe, some high official diplomatic characters more than hint at its truth.

5. Whether SIR A. MALET will have the kindness to afford his friends another opportunity of seeing the only acquaintance SIR ALEXANDER has ever brought with him to MARLBOROUGH, by name, as they understand, MR. SMALLCRAFT? Whether this be the same distinguished man who suffered so severely in the Courts of LOVE ?

6. Whether SIR A. MALET's principles are really of that benevolent and liberal character as to induce him to recommend his friends to support and deal with those alone who happen to agree with him in opinion ; and whether he does not consider that by so doing his friends may in all probability STARVE ?

An early answer will oblige, as many may wish to make further enquiries.

MARLBOROUGH,
5th. December, 1832

EMBERLIN AND HAROLD, PRINTERS, MARLBOROUGH.

CAUTION!!
The Burgesses
OF
MARLBOROUGH
ARE CAUTIONED AGAINST SIGNING THEIR
VOTING PAPERS
AT THE TOWN CLERK'S OFFICE,

Or under the direction of either of the Old Corporators, who are still anxiously seeking to retain possession of the BOROUGH PROPERTY, to the exclusion of the

RICHTFUL OWNERS,
The Inhabitants at large !!

December 19th, 1835.

W. W. LUCY, Printer, Post-Office, MARLBOROUGH.

INHABITANTS

OF

MARLBOROUGH.

The Mask is Withdrawn---
Truth must Prevail!!

You have now one of the grossest instances of misrepresentation laid open before you, that ever appeared in the Annals, even of Electioneering.

Compare the Charges made on the Case of that despicable Character, JORDAN, with the real Statement verified by the Attestation of all the respectable Gentlemen concerned, which is now in your Hands; and surely every honest man, however prejudiced, must shrink from a Cause that requires to be supported by such vile and slanderous Mis-statements.

Emberlin and Harold, Printers, Marlborough.

Above: A strongly worded poster from the 1830s. It is not clear if this refers to a parliamentary or a borough election.

Right: A spoof poster, in which borough election candidates are named and lampooned.

Opposite page: Three posters issued during the Parliamentary Elections of 1832. Despite numerous previous attempts to gain a seat, Sir Alexander Malet failed to oust either of the Tory candidates, one of whom was a member of the powerful Ailesbury family. Lord Ernest Bruce sat from 1832-1885, and Henry Bingham Baring from 1832-1867. The borough became part of the Devizes constituency in 1885.

1830.
Burderop Races.
TO BE RUN FOR
On the last day of the Races,
A PEWTER PLATE,
The Gift of T. G. ESTCOURT, and W. BANKES, Esqrs.
MEMBERS FOR MARLBOROUGH. CATCH WEIGHTS.

	HORSES.	RIDERS.	COLORS.
Mr. Wentworth's	Buck Pye by Savernake	A. Venison.	Gooseberry Green.
Field Marshall Brown's	Bruin out of Green Dragon.	Ino. Stupid.	Grass Green.
Mr. T. Merriman's	Coward by White Feather.	— Bully.	All Black.
Mr. I. Gardner's	Abuse by Gallipot.	— Jalap.	Yellow Breeches.
Mr. I. Russell's	Brass Fender out of Ironsides.	I. Steel.	Bronze.
Mr. T. Baverstock's	Blinker by Coward	A Boy	Brown.
Mr. T. Halcomb's	Pyeball by Skewball	T. Wheeler.	Drab.

Mr. I. Halcomb's Skewball, and Mr. I. Brinsden's Mealman, were named, but disqualified. Mr. B. Merriman's Whey and Curds, and Mr. C. Gregory's Bandbox, were not named in time.

All disputes to be settled by Stephen Brown, Esqr, Mayor of Marlborough, or by a Committee to be appointed.

☞ For the amusement of the Company, Coward will take the lead at starting in his Horse-Laugh.

Leaves from the Free Family Photograph Album

The following images are from an album dating from the 1920s. The Free family ran an important furniture and undertaking business, although they started in construction using sarsen stones. They moved to Marlborough from Hughenden, Buckinghamshire, in about 1850.

Above: Model T Ford tourer (fairly new, with a Bristol registration) decorated for Pewsey Carnival in 1922. The verse on the hood reads: 'When from Marlborough we come a-stealing, 'tis then we get the Kruschen feeling!' Posters flanking the car's radiator show a happy lady and gentleman supping the health-giving salts.

Above left: General Election, May 1929. Granny
Free is awaiting her car to the polling station.
She survived until the age of 104 – the Frees are
noted for their longevity.

Above right: Returning from the poll. Grannie
Free is having a chat with Mr Hurd, the MP for
the constituency.

Right: Wiltshire Agricultural Show, 3 June
1924. Worthies of the county: the mayor of
Marlborough, Alderman Thomas Free, is flanked
by the mayors of Swindon (left) and Devizes
(right). (Photograph by Hunt of Marlborough)

Opposite below: Part of the Free premises,
Nos 104–107 High Street, decorated for the visit
of the Duke of Connaught, 1925. The Duke was
opening Marlborough College Memorial Hall
which commemorates those old Marlburians
who died in the First World War. A flag was a flag
in those days.

Above: Alderman Thomas Free, six times mayor of Marlborough, standing by the soon-to-be demolished weighbridge, *c.* 1924. Most photographs show Alderman Free accompanied by his dog. The road has not yet been metalled.

Town criers' contest, 1914, in the Assembly Room of the town hall. Stout and other drinks have been served to the participants who betray no obvious signs of enjoyment. To be fair, until the 1920s it was considered undignified to smile or grin at the camera. The mayor, Mr E.N. Colbran, is in the middle at the back. The room has remained mercifully unchanged except for the loss of the fine pendant gasoliers. One wonders where and how the Windsor chairs were stored, predating the invention of the stacking chair as they do.

Opposite below: Town criers' competition, 1913. Although in poor condition, this image is interesting as it shows a throng of people in motion rather than posed. The photographer clearly possessed an up-to-date camera with a fast shutter speed.

Veterans pose for an Empire Day photograph, 1911.

Possibly Empire Day celebrations outside the town hall, *c.* 1910. On the balcony to the right a photographer uses a full-plate camera as the town council emerges.

Leaves from the Archive of the Late Ted Beauchamp

The following three photographs are from the archive of the late Ted Beauchamp, mayor in 1975 and 1976.

Beating the bounds. The mayor is in his bobble hat and to the left is Cllr A.V. Gray, mayor in 1972 and 1990, with his son Jeremy.

The mayoral party opening the Little Mop fair. A good time is being had by all.

Patrick Moore and Ted Moult recording *Treble Chance* in the Ailesbury Arms Hotel. There was no problem with smoking in those days.

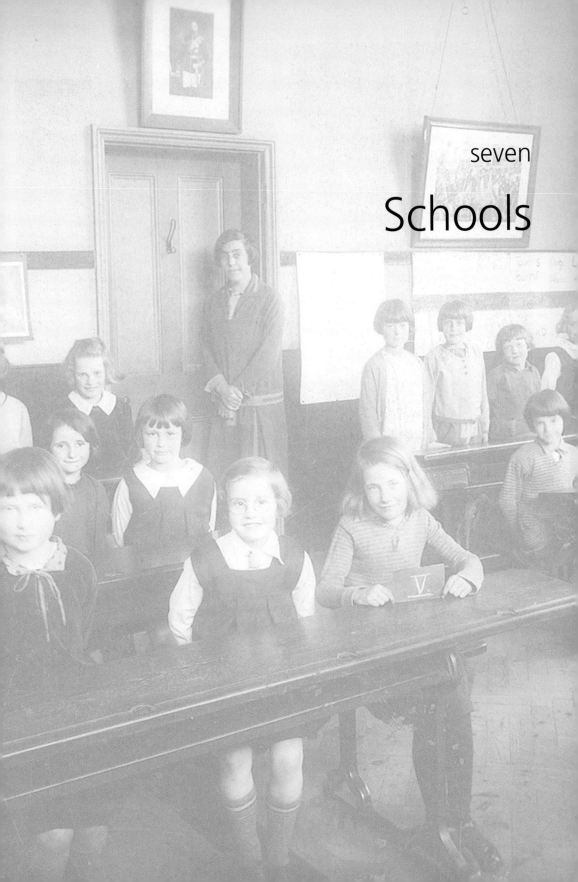

seven

Schools

Meet of the Tedworth Hunt at Tottenham House, April 1930. The little girl facing the camera is the author's mother.

Above: Mr Bristow's class, St Peter's boys' school, 1952. The building, now the public library, had changed little since Victorian times. Classrooms were heated by coke stoves, lavatories were outside in the yard shown. Canings were administered daily. The author is second from right in the third row from the top.

Right: The swinging sixties. This is the cover design for the grammar school's magazine. The mini-skirt has arrived.

Opposite below: The newly built grammar school, 1904; a finely detailed piece of architecture. To the left is Sebastopol Square, now destroyed, and to the right a part of the rope works.

Standard Five at St Mary's girls' school, *c.* 1930. Interior photographs of schools are unusual. A portrait of King George V hangs over the door.

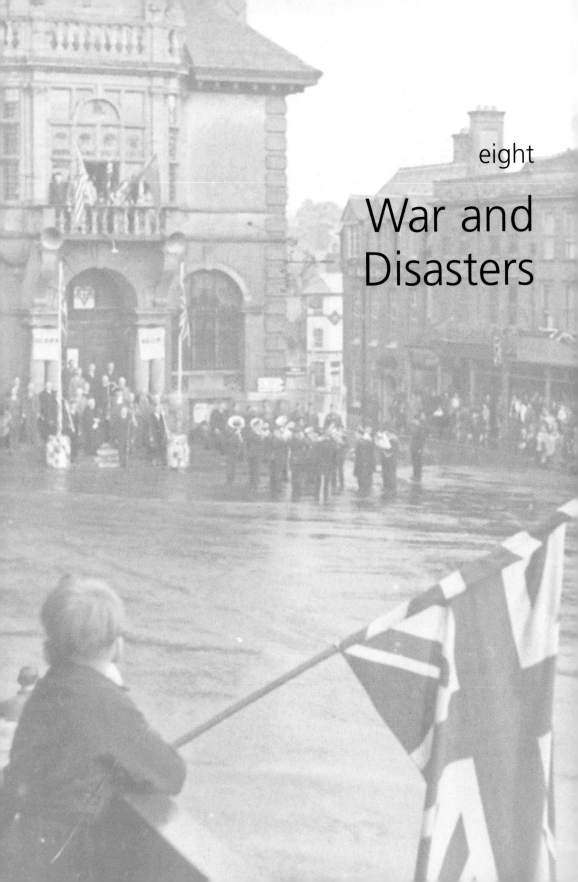

eight

War and Disasters

Above: Winter, 1914–15. Lorries en route to the Western Front fill the High Street.

Below: Army lorries in the High Street, 1914. The car to the right is a Model T Ford.

Above: An amazing sight in an age which saw only a handful of motor vehicles in the street at any one time (1914). Here the roadway is filled with military lorries, ambulances and cars. The hitching rail and flagpole were removed in 1929. The buildings have largely disappeared in the twentieth century. The first and third buildings were needlessly destroyed by developers; the second and fourth were destroyed by fire.

Right: A field service postcard sent from a war zone on 30 November 1915 by F. Bull of George Lane. The censor did not allow personal comments to be expressed.

NOTHING is to be written on this side except the date and signature of the sender. Sentences not required may be erased. If anything else is added the post card will be destroyed.

I am quite well.

I have been admitted into hospital.
{ sick } and am going on well.
{ wounded } and hope to be discharged soon.

I am being sent down to the base.

I have received your { letter dated *Nov 24*
{ telegram ,,
{ parcel ,,

Letter follows at first opportunity.

I have received no letter from you
{ lately.
{ for a long time.

Signature } *F. Bull*
only. }

Date *Nov 29 - 1915*

[Postage must be prepaid on any letter or post card addressed to the sender of this card.]

(25540) Wt.W3497-293 1,900m. 8/15 M.R.Co.,Ltd.

MC 74

Borough of Marlborough.

ZEPPELIN RAIDS.

In view of the possibility of Zeppelin Raids the inhabitants are requested from this date to diminish Lighting as much as possible, and to keep all blinds and curtains drawn.

Warning will be given of the approach of Zeppelins by sounding the Fire Alarm on the Town Hall 3 times in succession.

When the Alarm is sounded all Lights should be immediately extinguished, and everyone is strongly advised to remain indoors.

A. J. CROSBY, Mayor.
E. LLEWELLYN GWILLIM, Town Clerk.

2nd February, 1916.

"TIMES" PRINTING OFFICES, MARLBOROUGH.

Above: Artillery in the High Street, 1914–18.

Left: Procedures to be followed in the event of a Zeppelin raid, 1916.

Opposite above: A mock-up tank in the High Street taken outside the premises of Free's furnishers, 1918. To the left atop the tank is Donald Free, son of the proprietor.

Opposite below: Group photograph of the Home Guard, nursing staff and doctors, *c.* 1940. The young women, second row from the front, look very fetching in their tin hats.

INVASION EXERCISE

MARLBOROUGH

THIS exercise has been arranged for SUNDAY, 31ST JANUARY, 1943, between the hours of 8.30 and 5 o'clock and will be the biggest of the kind attempted in Marlborough. May I take the opportunity of emphasising the following points affecting the people of Marlborough as a whole?

Households living within 60—70 yards of Road Blocks are asked to make their contribution to the realism of the exercise by being ready to evacuate temporarily if required to do so. This does not mean that Military or Civil Defence Forces will enter the house or that everyone is expected to move out. But it is hoped that at any rate one person in each house (where there are more than this number) will be willing to come out, so that the W.V.S. can practice their arrangements for emergency feeding.

Those who move will be given a mid-day meal and will be told where to go when evacuated. They must not forget to take identity cards, gas masks, overcoats, and a blanket.

Everybody in the Borough should be ready to play their part in the exercise in the following ways :—

(a) To assist the Military and Civil Defence Forces to the utmost and to take part in incidents in their streets.
(b) To be ready to take into their houses temporarily people who have been evacuated.
(c) To keep off the streets when fighting is taking place in the Town and to avoid at all times standing about in groups.
(d) To keep in touch with the nearest Warden or Housewife.
(e) To refuse information to the enemy if interrogated.
(f) To rely for information on the Official Notice Boards at the following places :—

TOWN HALL
NATIONAL FIRE SERVICE DEPOT, LONDON ROAD
MARLBOROUGH COLLEGE
ST. PETER'S CHURCH
ST. THOMAS MORE R.C. CHURCH, ELCOT LANE.

* * * * *

The Exercise should not interfere with the normal Services at the various Places of Worship in the Town.

Yours faithfully,

F. J. HARRAWAY,
Chairman of Invasion Committee,
Borough of Marlborough.

N.B.—All BRITISH Forces will be wearing STEEL HELMETS. All " ENEMY " Soft Hats. All TANKS will be treated as " ENEMY."

1, The Green, Marlborough, Wilts,
January 28th, 1943.

Left: Notice of an invasion exercise, 1943.

Below: VE Day, 1945. The town celebrates the end of the Second World War on a rainy May Day.

Above: The same building as shown below. It is pictured here around 1910 when it belonged to Stephen Neate. The lower layers of roof retain the stone tiles which were widely used in Marlborough following the Great Fire of 1653. The brick walling is a later re-front on to timber framing. The properties in the centre and to the right are private houses; conversion to business use was to follow later.

Right: Dible and Roy's soft furnishing business at No. 34 High Street goes up in flames, 1976. The seventeenth-century timber-framed building was totally destroyed.

Fire strikes again, Nos 3 and 4 High Street on the morning after the serious blaze of 1998. Happily, the building is now fully restored.

nine

Recreation

Opposite above: Marlborough Amateur Dramatic and Operatic Society. The cast of *Rio Rita*, 1938. The annual production, complete with small orchestra, was staged in the town hall.

Opposite below: Marlborough Carnival, 1948. The lorry displays a host of awards, but for what?

Right: The first bathing place in Marlborough, Treacle Bolly in 1911. The swimmers appear to be in a state of panic.

Below: The swimming baths opened in 1923 and used unheated water from the river Kennet. It has since been lost to a housing development.

SWIMMING BATHS, MARLBOROUGH

Marlborough Town Football Club players in the 1916–27 season.

Marlborough Model Aircraft Club, Rockley Downs, *c.* 1950. A popular hobby in the 1950s and 1960s; many of the models were bought in kit form from Duck's Toy Shop in the High Street, one of the few family businesses which are still in existence.

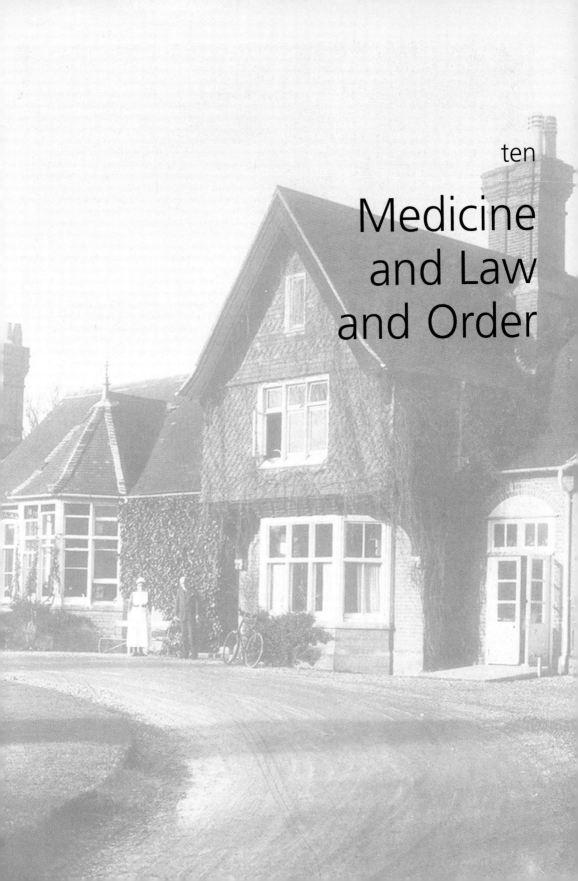

ten

Medicine
and Law
and Order

Savernake Cottage Hospital. Opened in 1872, it was designed by Sir George Gilbert Scott R.A. and built on land given by George Frederick, Marquess of Ailesbury. The accommodation consisted of two large wards with bathrooms attached, two smaller wards for isolation cases, two convalescent day rooms, an operating and consulting room, matron's sitting room and bedroom, servants' rooms, kitchen, scullery, laundry and wash house, stabling, carriage shed and mortuary. The photograph shows the building in 1929, the date of the Austin Seven car parked outside.

Savernake Hospital. Reproduction from the front cover of the centennial leaflet of 1996.

Above: Savernake Hospital. The nurses' recreational hall, 1966. The nurses are wearing their uniforms even when relaxing at table tennis.

Right: A fine example of typography from the printing works of Emberlin & Harold, High Street. Rewards for the recovery of stolen goods or apprehension of felons always seem disproportionately high in relation to wages.

5 POUNDS REWARD.

LOST,

(SUPPOSED TO BE STOLEN,)

On Friday Night the 10th, or early on Saturday Morning, the 11th of February, from a Farm Yard at Oare, in the Parish of Wilcot, Wilts, a Bright-Bay

GALLOWAY,

about 14 hands high, aged, long in the back, lame in the near leg behind, both knees broken, and used to go in harness.

Whoever will give such Information as may lead to the recovery of the said Galloway, shall, if stolen, receive the above Reward, on Conviction of the Offender or Offenders; and if strayed, shall be handsomely paid for their trouble and expences, on application to the REV. M. H. GOODMAN, Oare, *near* Pewsey, Wilts.

February 13th, 1832.

EMBERLIN & HAROLD, PRINTERS, HIGH-STREET, MARLBOROUGH.

Tottenham Park
ASSOCIATION,

For the Protection of Persons and Property, and for the Prosecution of Felons and other Offenders,

Extending over the Parishes of Burbage, Collingbourn Kingston, Collingbourn Ducis, Great Bedwin, Little Bedwin, Shalbourn, Easton, Preshute and Mildenhall, and over Savernake Forest and Park, in the County of Wilts.

THE FOLLOWING

REWARDS

Are allowed by this Association to any Person or Persons, not Members, giving Information of, and apprehending, any Offender or Offenders, who shall have committed any of the offences hereinafter mentioned, upon the Person or Property of any of the Members, (the Person informing to receive one half, and the Person apprehending such Offender or Offenders to receive the other half,) over and above all Rewards allowed by Act of Parliament, *viz.*:—

	£	s.	d.
MURDER, Highway, or Footpad Robbery, Burglary, or Housebreaking,			
Setting Fire to any Building, Hay, Corn, or other Effects, or	20	0	0
Stealing or Maiming any Horse, Mare, Gelding, Bull, Ox, Cow, Sheep or Lamb,			
Stealing or Maiming any Calf or Pig,	10	0	0
Stealing Corn, thrashed or unthrashed, or Hay, Poultry, Iron-Work, or Tackle belonging to any Implement of Husbandry, or from any Buildings or Gates,			
Any other Offence amounting to Felony, not hereinbefore mentioned,	5	0	0
Receiving Property of any description, knowing it to have been Stolen,			
Barking, Cutting, or Damaging Trees,			
Breaking Down or Stealing Gates, Pales, Posts, Rails, Wall Coping, or Hurdles,	3	3	0
Robbing any Orchard or Garden, or Destroying the Growth or Produce thereof,			
Breaking down or Stealing Wood or Underwood,			
Breaking and Stealing Dead Hedges,			
Stealing Straw or Haulm,	1	1	0
Stealing Turnips, Potatoes, or other Vegetables, Seeds or Grass, or putting Cattle to feed thereon,			

And by Rule XIII, the several Members of this Society, pledge themselves not to suffer within their respective Parishes, GIPSIES OR OTHER VAGRANTS to remain in the Lanes or other open Places; and the sum of FIVE SHILLINGS is allowed to any Person or Persons who shall Remove any Camp or Company of Gipsies out of the said Parishes.—Or in case any Member of this Society shall Prosecute such Gipsies or Vagrants, the Expence of such Prosecution shall be paid by the Society.

THO. B. MERRIMAN,
SOLICITOR TO THE SAID ASSOCIATION.

Marlborough, May 23rd, 1826.

R. EMBERLIN, PRINTER, MARLBOROUGH.

Anno Secundo
GULIELMI & MARIÆ.

An Act to Prohibit the Covering of Houses and other Buildings with Thatch or Straw, in the Town of *Marlborough* in the County of *Wilts.*

Hereas of late Years several sudden and dreadful Fires have happened within the Town of Marlborough in the County of Wilts, and particularly two Fires in the Month of April in the Year of our Lord, One thousand six hundred and ninety, whereby great numbers of Houses were consumed and burned down, or otherwise destroyed or demolished; Which Fires were occasioned, and the Damage thereby done much increased, by reason of Houses and other

A 2   Build-

BOROUGH OF
MARLBOROUGH.

MUCH Mischief and frequent Breaches of the Peace having been lately committed by idle & disorderly Persons at late Hours of the Night,— The Magistrates hereby require all *Publicans to take Notice,* that if they shall keep open their Houses, by permitting Persons to tipple therein, (or for any other purpose than the reception of Travellers,) after Ten o'Clock at Night, contrary to the Conditions of their Recognizances, proceedings at Law will be immediately instituted against them.

John Halcomb, Jun.
TOWN CLERK.

Above left: The Tottenham Park Association; a poster from 1826 showing an interesting tariff of values placed upon crimes.

Above right: Following fires in 1653, 1679 and 1690, the Act prohibiting the thatching of houses in the borough was eventually passed in this latter year, during the reign of William and Mary.

Left: How little things have changed! Trouble at closing time notice, *c.* 1825.

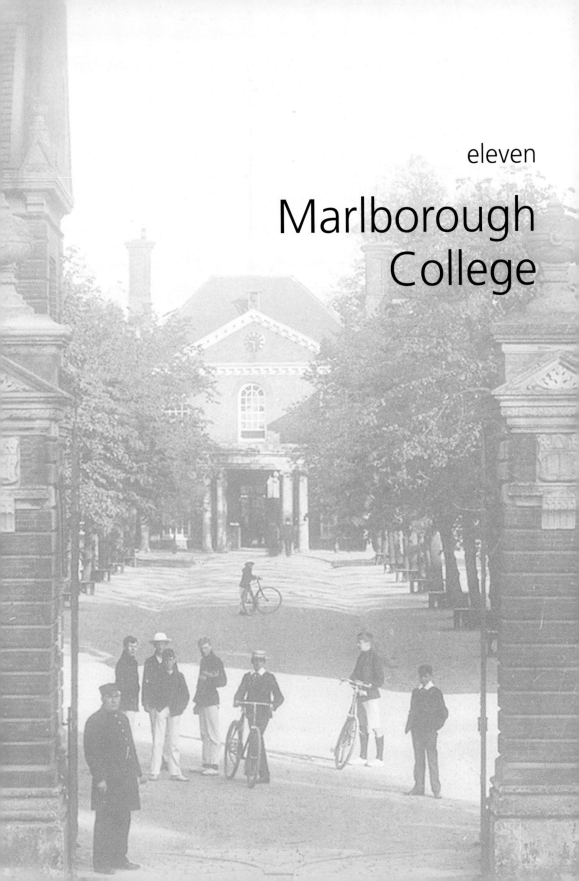

eleven

Marlborough College

A fine bird's-eye view of Marlborough College. This was the work of Christopher Hughes.

Aerial view of Marlborough College, 1925-1933. The large gardens in the foreground are now occupied by housing.

Marlborough College Cricket Pavilion, built in 1874 and still in use.

Marlborough College chapel designed in 1848 by architect Edward Blore. This was replaced by the present chapel of St Michael and all Angels in 1886. To the front can be seen the porter's lodge of 1877-87. (Alfred Seeley, Richmond Hill, Surrey)

College gates, pre–1887. (Jones, photographer, Marlborough)

Marlborough College gates, 1916. Some of the boys are wearing summer-issue boaters. The college porter, Mr Shepherd, in his quasi-military uniform, was in post from 1910–1935. He never missed a photo opportunity.

The porter's lodge footbridge (1910) and chancel of the chapel, Marlborough College, mid-1920s.

Marlborough College quad in the 1920s. The trees and central road were removed around 1955. On the right the lower building is the old dining hall now replaced by the 1960s Norwood Hall.

Marlborough College quad, *c.* 1880. On the left are open-air fives courts, replaced by the north block in 1893.

Marlborough College 'C' house, originally built for the sixth Duke of Somerset, *c.* 1699–1720. This was at one time the Castle Inn.

A postcard entitled 'Marlborough College, New Building' dates this precisely to 1910.

The modernist science buildings of Marlborough College, 1933. Surprisingly, the classical Memorial Hall of 1925, seen to the left, was designed by the same architect, Ernest Newton.

Marlborough College bathing place, *c.* 1920. The curved shape is explained by its forming part of the moat of Marlborough Castle. It has recently been filled in and built upon.

twelve

Coronation
Day

Jim Dunford's record of Coronation Day, 1953. These form part of a fine collection of 100 pictures taken by Mr Dunford, a professional photographer. Apart from the events taking place, they are an invaluable record of buildings, clothing and other details. Even the food provided for the tea party is clearly identifiable, a boon for social historians.

Opposite above: The whole town turned out for the celebrations.

Opposite below: The Coronation mugs have been collected from the mayor, Alderman Eric J. Free and are triumphantly borne aloft. How did parents persuade schoolboys to wear uniform on occasions such as this? The Ailesbury Arms hotel balcony is still shrouded in cement; this was later removed to reveal the original cast-iron balustrading.

Right: Two young men take the presentation of their mugs very seriously. Notice the fashion for Prince Charles coats.

Below: Country dancing outside the Castle & Ball Hotel.

The tea party. Enjoyment is expressed in a variety of ways.

Senior citizens at tea; the older women cling to the fashion of wearing hats.

An impressively large crowd awaits an historical pageant in the grounds of Marlborough College.

The pageant begins.

A young actor from the pageant poses outside 'C' house at the college.

Opposite above: Coronation Day, 1953. The civic procession is led by the carnival queen and her attendants.

Opposite below: A combination of Wiltshire's famous product and the stubbornness of its inhabitants, 1913.

A Wiltshire Pig.

You may push me
You may shuv
But I'm hanged
If I'll be druv
From Marlborough.

Other local titles published by Tempus

Chippenham Memories
RUTH MARSHALL

Compiled from the recordings of the Chippenham Voices Oral History Project, this book brings together the personal memories of people who have lived and worked in the market town of Chippenham, vividly recalling childhood and schooldays, sport and leisure, the war years and working life. Illustrated with 100 personal photographs and archive images drawn from the Chippenham Museum and Heritage Centre, *Chippenham Memories* offers a unique glimpse of the past.

0 7524 3511 6

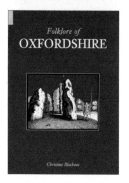

Folklore of Oxfordshire
CHRISTINE BLOXHAM

This fascinating illustrated study of folklore rediscovers those traditions that have either vanished, been ignored or hidden away, such as the lore relating to the Rollright Stones and Wayland's Smithy. There are tales of poaching and highwaymen, but always at the heart of Oxfordshire's folklore are the traditional beliefs, stories, events and customs of the common people. *Folklore of Oxfordshire* will be of interest to all those who wish to revel in the delights of times past.

0 7524 3664 3

Cirencester at War
PETER GRACE

Cirencester at War is a pictorial record of the main events of the Second World War as they impacted on the town of Cirencester and its surrounding district. Illustrated with over 200 old photographs and documents, the book gives an insight into wartime life with its tragedy, heroism, austerity and, of course, humour. This book recalls an important era in Cirencester's history and will bring back wartime memories for many people.

0 7524 3477 2

Haunted Oxford
ROB WALTERS

Drawing on historical and contemporary sources *Haunted Oxford* contains a chilling range of ghostly accounts. From tales of spirits that haunt the libraries of the Oxford Colleges and shades that sup at the pubs and watering holes around the city, to stories of spectral monks and even royal ghosts, this phenomenal gathering of ghostly goings-on is bound to captivate anyone interested in the supernatural history of the area.

0 7524 3925 1

If you are interested in purchasing other books published by Tempus, or in case you have difficulty finding any Tempus books in your local bookshop, you can also place orders directly through our website

www.tempus-publishing.com